ON TRIAL
A TEST OF MY FAITH

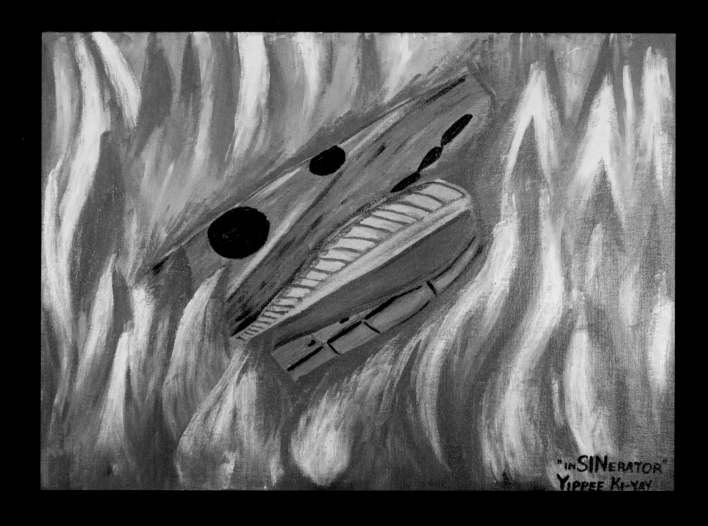

"inSINerator"
Yippee Ki-Yay

KOLLIN L. TAYLOR

Cover art by Kollin L. Taylor

AuthorHouse™
1663 Liberty Drive
Bloomington, IN 47403
www.authorhouse.com
Phone: 833-262-8899

Because of the dynamic nature of the Internet, any web addresses or links contained in this book may have changed since publication and may no longer be valid. The views expressed in this work are solely those of the author and do not necessarily reflect the views of the publisher, and the publisher hereby disclaims any responsibility for them.

Any people depicted in stock imagery provided by Getty Images are models, and such images are being used for illustrative purposes only.
Certain stock imagery © Getty Images.

This book is printed on acid-free paper.

ISBN: 978-1-4918-7450-9 (sc)
ISBN: 978-1-4918-7451-6 (e)

Print information available on the last page.

Library of Congress Control Number: 2014905199

Published by AuthorHouse 03/16/2022

authorHOUSE®

"inSINerator"

2021

Acrylic on canvas

11 × 14

by Kollin L. Taylor

Setting the Captive Free
September 4, 2020
Acrylic on paper
22 × 28
by Kollin L. Taylor

CONTENT

Dedication 5

Acknowledgments 7

Introduction 9

Iron Curtain 10

Tested Alone......................11

In the Face of Defeat 12

The Trial 13

Hostile Witness..................15

The Bounty........................16

Bail Bondsman...................17

Jailbait 18

Eleventh Hour....................19

Hard to Tell 20

Life without Parole 21

Presidential Appeal 22

Up His Sleeve.................... 23

God's Attorney.................. 24

God's Message.................. 25

Withholding Evidence 26

Waiting Period.................. 27

The Sky 28

Mud in My Eyes................ 29

Sweet Blessing 30

Two Wrongs 31

Red Sea.............................32

Life Savings......................33

DOA? No Way! 34

The Visionary 35

Never Late 36

My Own 37

Like Elijah......................... 38

Graduation Day (Higher
Authority) 39

Sealed 40

Under Attack......................41

The Process 42

Inception........................... 43

Rod and Reel 44

Part Two............................ 45

Faith 46

Faithful Service................. 47

Not by Sight...................... 48

So Much 49

Stop.................................. 50

Details 51

Rusted Hope......................52

No Doubt 53

About The Author............. 54

DEDICATION

To the woman the LORD God ordained as my wife. I do not know how or when the Heavenly Father will bring us together, but based on my journey thus far, I know it will be special when He does. I am looking forward to our journey together.

ACKNOWLEDGMENTS

Heavenly Father, since this journey began, the amount of emotional pain I have endured exceeds the pain I have experienced throughout the rest of my life. You have stretched me beyond my perceived limits, and You keep stretching me. By Your grace, my faith is much bigger than a mustard seed, yet You continually put me to the test to induce additional growth. Thanks for the teachers You used to help me along my journey of spiritual growth, especially Your Son Jesus Christ and Holy Spirit. Even though I dedicated *On Trial: A Test of My Faith* to the woman You ordained as my wife, I know the gift is never as important as You, the Giver. Heavenly Father, thank You for Your blessings that I cannot even begin to numerate.

Sterlin King, thank you very much for your generosity.

Update: One of the reasons for revising the 2014 edition of *On Trial: A Test of My Faith* is to remove the previous painting from the front cover. That painting from 2013 was of me in the "furnace of affliction" (Isaiah 48:10-11). But the time has come for the tormentors to get tormented. The Lord inspired me to do the new painting based on a vision He showed me of an evil spirit, which He dubbed: *Not my rib. Never were, never will be. I never knew you. Depart from me, you worker of iniquity!* The evil spirit is in the form of a locust that is experiencing God's justice in the lake of fire and brimstone (see Revelation 9:1-11, 20:10). Hence the name, *"inSINerator"*, which is linked to the new painting on the rear cover. The locust also serves as a reminder of when the Lord said to me, "I will restore unto you all the years the locust has eaten."

INTRODUCTION

A Test of My Faith poetically and prophetically reveals an epic part of my life's story. Consequently, it is not *an ex post facto* testimony of how the LORD God delivered me. *On Trial: A Test of My Faith* is about God's sufficient grace to preserve me during an intense and extended trial where He tested and refined me, particularly my faith and patience (James 1:3-4).

In 2013, an Army Chaplain said I reminded him of King David. I initially thought it was because I was a writer and a poet. However, I felt more like Job due to his sufferings. I soon discovered what the Lord had used the Chaplain to convey to me. The Lord anointed David to replace the rebellious King Saul, but David had to wait for years before the fulfillment of the Lord's promise. The future king endured several threats against his life including exile, and King Saul giving David's wife Michal to another man. David also endured numerous tests to his faith in God prior to his kingship. I can relate to what King David wrote in Psalm 66:9-12 because the LORD God has tested and refined me like silver, in the furnace of affliction. As far as I know, the Lord did not anoint me as an earthly king, and neither am I in a "place of abundance". But I have faith that God will fulfill His promises to me in accordance with Luke 1:37.

I would be remiss if I did not mention that, despite my faith, there were many times—regardless of what God had waiting for me on the other side—when I wanted to die rather than suffer for another day. Therefore, I frequently lamented like Job. Interestingly, I felt as if my preexisting elevated level of faith made the process even more difficult. This is what Jesus said about what the Heavenly Father does to make the fruitful even more productive for His glory:

> "I AM the True Vine, and My Father is the Husbandman. Every branch in Me that beareth not fruit He taketh away: **and every branch that beareth fruit, He purgeth it, that it may bring forth more fruit.**" ~ John 15:1-2

> (King James Version)

I knew the LORD God could give me a breakthrough in an instant, but, instead, I either received a break from the turmoil or found encouragement to continue going through the process. Sometimes He graciously strengthened me so I felt as if I could continue suffering like this for the rest of my life. But then there are times when I wanted God to quickly end it one way or another. Hebrews 11 is a chronicle of people whose faith in God were put to extreme tests. Likewise, my faith in the LORD God was tested beyond my imagination. I have had to endure hardness as a soldier of Christ Jesus, and so just as the Lord told the Apostle Paul, His grace was sufficient for me, particularly when my questions outnumbered the answers.

Prayerfully, *On Trial: A Test of My Faith* will help you endure the challenges you will face when your faith in God is tested. Never forget that the sufferings in this life are temporary. In addition, they are incomparable to your rewards from the Lord Jesus, and that you can do all things through Christ Jesus who strengthens you.

Iron Curtain

There is certainly no denial
That my faith is on trial.
Every day, I blaze a trail
That makes it seem as if I'll fail.
But there's one thing for certain:
God typically works from behind an iron curtain.

Most of the time, we can't see
The wonderful things that will come to be.
He will make us happy and proud
When He removes the shroud.

So, while you see that I will fail,
I see that the Lord will prevail.
Before the LORD God fulfills a desire,
He sometimes tries us with fire.

Tested Alone

This trial will test me down to the bone.
Plus, I'll have to go through it alone.
Absent loving support, for which I yearn,
I'll have to go alone when it's my turn.
It's good to have earthly love night and day,
But I'll have to travel alone with the Lord for the rest of the way.

In the Face of Defeat

Even though the fire will bring the heat,
Jesus is the attorney no one can beat.
Nothing but the truth in God's courtroom is the rule.
With Jesus as my attorney, victory is assured, but I must keep cool.
Regardless of the high heat,
I must praise the Lord Jesus, especially in the face of defeat.

The Trial

The Heavenly Father was the Judge. He called the court to order.
The devil was the "persecuting attorney" on the other side of the border.
The devil brought evidence and witnesses from all over the place.
I couldn't believe that liar kept a straight face!

Jesus cross-examined the witnesses like a broom,
Sweeping their lies out of the courtroom.
He searched everyone's heart down to the root,
And then He extracted the lies and the truth.

The evidence stacked against me delivered a vicious blow,
But Jesus slowly used the truth to cut my opponents down low.
Yet, the devil felt great, so he confidently pounded his chest.
Then both attorneys gave the case a rest.

The jury of twelve apostles received no introductions,
But the Judge gave them His instructions.
The jurors left for their deliberation,
Which seemed like the beginning of my tribulation.

My trial left me feeling beaten and feeble.
My seat was hard and sharp, as if I was sitting on a needle.
The trial left me feeling as if I had been pelted with dung.
Maybe the case will be dismissed because the jury is hung.

I heard all the chatter in the courtroom.
I was as nervous as a waiting groom.
I could feel the sweat dripping down into my socks
As I watched the seconds tick off the clocks.
Every second seemed more like an hour,
But this trial was to demonstrate the Lord's mercy, grace, and power.

I looked around at everyone I could see,
But only the Lord Jesus Christ could help me.
I leaned forward and began to pray.
My freedom was blocked, but Jesus was the Way.

Then came the decisive moment when I had to face my fear:
The door opened and the jury of apostles started to appear.
I wondered if history was about to be repeated.
My legs were so weak that I wanted to stay seated.
Then I saw the devil as he looked over my way.
I read his lips. "Guilty" was all he had to say.
Then I felt the touch of the angel of death
As I smelled the sulfur of the devil's breath.

I started smiling as the devil turned very red
When the words "Not guilty!" were said.
I was freed from the affliction that was eating away at my soul
Because I had submitted to the Lord Jesus, giving Him full control.

Despite everything the devil had up his sleeve,
I didn't succumb to his efforts to deceive.
The Judge immediately proclaimed I was free to go.
I hugged and thanked Jesus and left with a heavenly glow.

As the devil started heading out with a sneaky walk,
The Judge called him to the chambers so they could talk.
The entire courtroom erupted in an audible sigh
Because the devil was about to get it. Oh yeah, that's why.

As I was leaving the courtroom after surviving this strife,
I saw that the next defendant was my future wife.

Hostile Witness

I thought my trial put me through hell,
But knowing my beloved was on trial didn't sit well.
I knew that her attorney knew His stuff,
But I also knew that the devil would get rough.
This was a test of my spiritual fitness,
Especially when the devil called me as a hostile witness.
I know I promised to tell nothing but the truth,
But the devil's questions knocked out a tooth.
I knew that I was under oath,
But it really hurt when the devil hit me in my throat.

Thank goodness that, before it was too late,
Jesus cross-examined me and set the record straight.
I looked over at my beloved with a smile.
As I left the courtroom, I said to her, "I'll see you outside in a while."

What I heard shortly after made perfect sense.
The Judge dismissed the case on grounds of insufficient evidence.

The Bounty

Recently found not guilty, now I'm on the run,
As the devil chases me with a gun.
Just when I thought my life was heaven-sent,
The devil refuses to relent.

I walk with the Lord Jesus, yet, every day and night,
I am locked in with a devil for spiritual a fight.
Even when I go beyond this county,
For my soul, the devil offers a bounty.

I am about to snap!
The sneaky devil caught me in a trap!

Bail Bondsman

Hello, my dear Lord Jesus. I need help with the bail.
The devil has me in his jail.
By the way, we need You.
I say we because he has a few more, too.
Unfortunately, they didn't know what to do.
Most had forgotten how to reach You.
So, I told them to close their eyes and bow,
And then I showed them how.
Now they know that for any trial,
It is good to keep You, sweet Jesus, on speed dial.

Jailbait

Calm down, fellas. I know I called yesterday, and now it's half past noon,
But the Lord Jesus is coming. He is coming very soon.
...I know that it has been a few days,
But while you've complained, have you worked on changing your ways?
The Lord Jesus is coming, and we will get bailed,
But if you return here, it will be like He failed.
If that were to happen, He may keep coming back,
But after a while, He won't cut you any slack.
He has been waiting on you for the last few days,
But you first must strengthen your holy ways.

Eleventh Hour

You just complained that you made an emergency call
And the Lord Jesus Christ didn't answer you at all.
There's one thing about every single word
You said: He heard.
I know it is the eleventh hour,
But it's the perfect time for Jesus to demonstrate His power.
Say He lets it go all the way.
Sometimes, that's the price you must pay.
Even if He doesn't rescue you from this mess,
It doesn't mean that He loves you any less.
Sometimes, when we go through something rough,
It's because we need a love that's tough.
Then there are times when to show He's great,
Jesus works a miracle when we think it's too late.

Hard to Tell

Sometimes, it's so hard to tell
The difference between Earth and hell.
Even when things are going well,
It's still hard to know if I'm on Earth or in hell.

I can usually find trouble lurking close by
When good news has me flying high.
When blessings inflate my joy like a balloon,
The devil usually stops by real soon.

It's not for a lack of trying
That sometimes I don't know if I'm alive or dying.
Sometimes, it's so hard to tell
The difference between Earth and hell

Life without Parole

This is way out of my control:
I'm an innocent man sentenced to life without parole.
But to show that He is great,
Jesus freed me from behind the steel gate.
The end to my sentence was abrupt
Because my prosecutor was corrupt.
There were so many times that he lied
And so many people who died.

So, even though this was out of my control,
The Lord Jesus took my place and saved my soul.

Presidential Appeal

All day, I sat and cried,
Because yesterday I should've died.
I thought I was going to take my last breath
After being sentenced to death.
But it was all so you could see
How the Lord Jesus was going to rescue me.

It was hard not to squeal
After my denied appeal.
Then I got the word from the warden;
I had received a Presidential pardon.
I later found out that the President had been trying to sleep
When a dream woke her up and caused her to weep.
She couldn't go back to sleep at all
Until she made that phone call.

It was the Lord Jesus, for sure,
Because she had never heard of me or my case before.

Up His Sleeve

The devil has a lot up his sleeve
To try to derail what I might achieve.
But Jesus is simply putting my faith on show.
I don't just believe; I know!

God's Attorney

At some point along the journey,
We may feel like we are the Lord's attorney.
We may even ask why
He let someone die.
But there's one thing about me and you:
We don't have a clue.
We only make God laugh.
He's the only one who sees the world's entire photograph.
We cannot argue why.
We can only testify.
We don't see His face,
But we can attest to His grace.
He'll put us on a shelf
So that He can speak for Himself.
Sometimes, for others to live, someone else must die.
An organ donation may be a part of the reason why.
Sometimes, death can motivate
Us to spread love instead of hate.
When we are scratched by the devil's claw,
We may end up with something like Megan's Law.[1]
When alcohol makes us sad,
Someone forms MADD.[2]

So, for the rest of my life's journey,
I am God's witness; He does not need an attorney.
There're so many things that happen. No matter how we try,
Only God can tell us the real reasons why.

[1] Megan's Law, which addresses sex offenders and child molesters, was signed by President Clinton on May 17, 1996. Megan's Law was much needed, despite Washington State's 1990 Community Protection Act, which included America's first law authorizing public notification when dangerous sex offenders are released into the community. It was the brutal 1994 rape and murder of seven-year-old Megan Kanka by a previously registered sex offender that prompted the public demand for broad-based community notification (**http://www.megans-law.net/.** Accessed July 5, 2013).

[2] "Founded by a mother whose daughter was killed by a drunk driver, Mothers Against Drunk Driving® (MADD) is the nation's largest nonprofit working to protect families from drunk driving and underage drinking. MADD also supports drunk and drugged driving victims and survivors at no charge, serving one person every eight minutes through local MADD victim advocates and at 1-877-MADDHELP" (**http://www.madd.org/about-us/.** Accessed July 5, 2013).

God's Message

When God has a message for you,
Nothing's going to stop it from getting through.
A sent e-mail may fail,
But a message from God will always prevail.

We can go in a cave and hide,
Only to find that God is waiting inside.
We can spend all day avoiding the fire,
But our dreams reveal our deepest desire.

We can stay busy and, on the go,
But we can't reject God's messages and expect to grow.
The memories He created, we cannot rewrite.
To try to forget them is a losing plight.

Withholding Evidence

This is not an indictment
About my lack of enlightenment.
The only thing that makes sense
Is that the Lord is withholding evidence.
That's why I'm so certain
That He does things behind an iron curtain.

While I'm here with a bad feeling,
I know Jesus is there doing some healing.
There're signs all around,
Yet no clues can be found.
You might know that others have a clue,
But no one's telling you.
It's like having a mate who puts on a show
When you are the last one to know.
Your family and friends had a clue,
But absolutely no one told you.
Sometimes, they had no idea how you would react
If they were to share that disturbing fact.
It's like falling in love with someone who has braids,
But no one told you that she has AIDS.
Because, like a flaming bullet from gun,
You probably would've taken off and run.
But the Lord wanted you to give that person a chance,
Because she's still deserving of romance.
That person deserves love, too.
The truth is, so do you.

So, now it makes perfect sense
Why the Lord sometimes withholds evidence.
Before we put a sour look on our face,
We must remember that we are here because of God's grace.

Waiting Period

By the Lord Jesus Christ I was anointed,
But there was a time when I was disappointed.
My disappointment clearly showed in my gait.
I didn't know my journey would include this long and painful wait.
Sometimes, in my tears I would drown,
But then I remembered how long it took David to wear his crown.
David had to wait until it was his God-appointed day,
And for the LORD God to remove King Saul from out of his way.
Take matters into his hands? David never dared.
Each day he spent waiting was a day getting prepared.

So, I'll patiently wait after my anointment
For the day when God approves my appointment.

The Sky

The sun is always in the sky.
Have you ever wondered why?
Even when it's dark, ten hours past noon,
The sun will reappear soon.
Even when darkness hits your life strong,
The darkness will not last long.
Things will eventually get bright
Because the Lord already said, "Let there be light!"

And even when it's twelve hours past noon,
The dark sky is usually lit by the moon.
The sun and moon also demonstrate,
Jesus is always present so we must have faith.

Other things won't have a time that's set,
But trusting the Lord Jesus is a decision you will never regret.

Mud in My Eyes

Jesus placed mud in my eyes
And I was blinded. But that was no surprise.
It was done for the best,
As it also gave my faith a test.
He did it for my healing,
But that's not what I'm feeling.
People look at me and laugh
As I wear God's autograph.

The way is not something I can see,
But I know the Lord Jesus is paving it for me.
So, while my eyes can't see,
My faith tells me that the Lord Jesus Christ is leading me.

And for those who are looking and laughing at me,
Keep looking, because there's something special Jesus wants you to see.

Sweet Blessing

The Lord didn't make this easy for me.
With mud in my eyes, I couldn't see.
Yet, He sent me down this road
To get rid of my load.
Even when I tried to cry,
My tears didn't wash away the mud pie.

Part of my anointment,
Is this mud that is more like an ointment.
Jesus simply told me to go
And listen for the blessings to flow.

The Lord wanted me to taste the sweetness by taking a sip.
Then, He wanted me to take a dip.
Jesus took me by my hand. This is what He had to say:
"Follow Me, I AM the Way."

My heart started to smile
When I heard the blessings flow after a while.
I didn't let any go to waste
As my lips gave the sweet blessings a taste.
It was only the beginning of this trip
As Jesus led me into the pool of His endless love in for a dip.
It came as no surprise
When the blessing washed the ointment from my eyes.

Whenever I close my eyes, after this story,
I can still see God's awesome glory.

Two Wrongs

It may seem like a silly thing to do,
Being faithful to someone who isn't faithful to you.
But while the person may have fulfilled a desire,
You may get burned if you play with fi re.

Your punishments won't be the same,
And you may be left shooting a flame.
While your partner went and got wild,
You may conceive a child.

While you may have just parted ways,
That former partner stalks you for days.
So, just because someone does something to you
Doesn't mean that you should do the same thing, too.

Two wrongs don't make a right,
Especially in the heavenly Father's sight.
It's bad enough that everyone pays
Even when only one person sinfully plays.

But if you patiently wait,
The Lord Jesus will set everyone straight.

Red Sea

He forcefully parted my Red Sea
And deeply, repeatedly penetrated me.
This is a power struggle for my body and soul.
I fought, but he gained control.
"I wish this would be over quickly!" I said,
But the battle raged on instead.
I can't believe this is happening! circulated in my head.
Survival? No. I sought death instead.

After he had scared, violated, and scarred me,
He quit his pursuit so he could flee.
The tears from my soul flowed with the Red Sea
As I shamefully asked, "Why, dear Lord, did You let this happen to me?"
There was silence. The Lord Jesus didn't explain
Why my body and soul were filled with pain.
I never thought that my life was golden
Until what I had was stolen.

Life Savings

So many stories of rags to riches.
But then the people get too big for their britches.
Then, they go from riches to rags—
From dozing in mansions to sleeping in bags.

Some crawl back and regain riches,
While some are left with festering stitches.
It tests our faith to see evil people succeed,
Especially while Believers have an unmet need.

This may make some wonder if there's a God.
Others may give the devil a nod.
But be careful to whom you give your soul,
Because eternal life is the ultimate goal.

If giving your soul to the devil seemingly ends your strife,
Just wait until you see the interest you'll pay for the rest of your life.
With the Lord, every day your faith will get tested.
But you won't believe the incredible returns on what you've invested.

DOA? No Way!

Having faith is easier when you know Jesus will see you through,
But it's different when the one who needs Him is not you—
Like when a loved one is pronounced dead on arrival,
But your heart tells you there's a chance of survival.

Then, by a miracle, the person ends up in ICU.
There's not much you can do.
You listen to what the doctors have to say,
But you hear a different prognosis when you pray.

Even though cardiac arrest threatened my beloved's survival,
I am grateful Jesus was there for the revival.
So, the next time the doctors say DOA,
Check with the Lord Jesus to learn what He has to say.

The Visionary

The curse of a visionary is seeing what will or could be,
And then waking up to a cold, harsh reality.
Whether a vision, thought, or dream,
Things don't always appear as they seem.
Sometimes, I can't tell which is worse for me:
Walking around blindly or not getting what I see.

The visions leave a sweet taste,
But reality makes them seem like a waste.
God may show me how things are going to be,
But then withhold the dates from me.

Lord Jesus, I know You played a safe bet
When I begged for my blessing and You said, "Not yet."
I wanted to fulfill my destiny,
But You knew I lacked the maturity.
You also knew that a bit of deprivation
Would increase my level of appreciation.
You also knew that a blessing too soon down the road
Would end up being too heavy a load.
For You to fulfill my burning desires
Would flatten all four of my tires.
Moreover, the journey marked with futility
Was to instill the requisite humility.

The visions showed God's blessings that were great,
But now I know that I must wait.

Never Late

It was like tempting fate.
The Lord showed up late.
Jesus is always on time, so how could that be?
It turned out He had something for us to see.

My hopes and dreams were totally dead,
But Jesus showed up and got them out of bed.
I had heard about Lazarus, so this came as no surprise.
But, still, I could not believe my eyes!

I never lost faith, but doubt plagued this story.
Now I can see, so I testify for God's glory.

My Own

All I want is my own
To really set the tone.
I want to peacefully sleep
And to no longer weep.

Dear Lord Jesus, only You can close this distance,
And I know You can do it this instance.
You see my face buried in the dirt
And my heart filled with hurt.

Like Elijah

The Prophet Elijah had incredible power,
But I'm not talking about the time when he called down a fiery shower.
While my hopes and dreams fall,
It seems as if You always answered Elijah's call.
While I apparently cannot get through,
Elijah quickly received answers from You.

What can I do or say
For You to answer my prayers that way?
I know my prayers are not the same,
But the answer will still glorify Your name.

The king's men were destroyed by fi re,
But mine is a peaceful desire.
All I need to get out of this jail
Is a simple, yet special, e-mail.

There is nothing I can do
Because, like Elijah, I am powerless without You.

Graduation Day (Higher Authority)

Is today when I fulfill my fate?
Is today when I graduate?
I know I have much farther to go,
But, for now, is this the plateau?

Is today when Jesus confers the "Master's" degree,
Or does He have much more for me?
Thank You, Lord Jesus, for training me,
But I didn't know this was for a PhD.

Sealed

My fate has been sealed.
I rest in turmoil on my shield.
No last words to impart.
My sword is buried deep in my heart.
The last thought that entered my head
Was that God can raise the dead.

I tearfully made my plea,
But there's no telling if He is ignoring me.
I can imagine how Lazarus must have felt
About the hand he was dealt.
But from that experience, there's something I lack,
Because I'm still waiting to be brought back.

I heard the mourners say, "Be still and wait,"
But they're alive—and living's great.
My world is pitch-black,
And I'm entombed and covered in a sack.

Under Attack

Being a Christian doesn't mean being affliction-free.
Look at Paul, Job, and me.
I know those two are of historical fame,
While most have never heard my name.
But God also gets much glory
From my epic painful story.
A life filled with sunshine and rain,
With a little success, and deep-rooted in pain.
Away at my soul, the devil tries to rip.
Only God can right this ship.
As I continue to drift away,
I know the Lord Jesus has already saved the day.

The Process

My dear Heavenly Father, do You hear my plight?
Dealing with it causes me to write.
How much longer must I suffer in pain?
After these battles, will any part of me remain?
I know there's a divine purpose for Your plan,
Even Jesus experienced pain when He was a man.

There's only one thing that I seek,
The one thing that plagues me every week.
It makes the tears flow when I pray;
It saddens my soul every day.

Inception

Ever since time's inception,
We've been plagued by deception.
The devil does his part
To make us feel extra-smart.
He'll encourage us and say,
"You can do it and get away.
Go and put on a show.
Because you're smart, they'll never know."

He may play Truth or Dare,
But his goal is to ensnare.
He may add to God's gift and make you choose
Because he wants you to lose.
He is cunning and was there at time's start,
So he knows how to prey on the pride in your heart.
He'll lure you away from God with a bigger bone
So he can get you all alone.
But it will be your damnation
To succumb to his temptation.
What really adds to the delusion
Is the devil's tempting confusion.

Rod and Reel

There's something in my heart that I deeply feel.
I want that fish, but I need a special rod and reel.
Go ahead and look
At the end of the line: God is the hook.

It's going to be a long and hard fight today,
But I'm not letting you get away.
The rod is secure, and I'm strapped to my seat.
Catching this fish will be a miraculous feat.

I'll have to rely on God's incredible powers,
As I know this battle could go on for hours.
I'll start in the morning, and I'll hold on until it's night,
Because this is worth the wait and the fight.

The reason I'm using a fi shing line
Is because I can't use a net to catch the only fish that's mine.
The ocean sits wide and blue,
But God has only joined me and you.

Part Two

Every time I blow a fuse and vent,
I must turn around and repent.
This thorn in my side makes me weak.
Death or relief is what I seek.

The depths of my pain made me pray
And ask God for death rather than facing another day.
He knows the whole story, while I only have a clue.
It hurts worse when the same thing happens in part two.

I woke up to another day of grief.
I didn't die; there's still no relief!
Why is this my price to pay?
Why do I have to live like this another day?
To rebel is to fight a battle I cannot win,
And to express the depths of my pain would be a sin.

Times like these make me feel hated.
I am grateful for life but despise that I was created.
Lord, it's obvious that I am in distress.
I'm impatiently waiting . . . . When will You rescue me from this mess?

My Lord, I know that You can hear, see, and feel my grief,
Yet You withhold my relief.
It feels like such a calamity,
This test of my faith, patience, and humanity.

Faith

It takes faith to believe in a God you cannot see
Yet who won't let you practice idolatry.
It takes faith to believe in a God who closed doors on me,
Leading others to say, "I guess it wasn't meant to be."
But it's that faith in what I cannot see
That makes me believe the LORD God will perform an Abraham-and-Sarah miracle
for me.

Faithful Service

I went through things that made me a better man.
Then I said, "Did I get broken again, my Lord, because You can?"
I wondered how You could've broken me this much.
I'm the better man no one wanted to touch.

Darkness covered much of my recent story,
But it was all a part of Your plan for glory.
The glory wasn't intended for me.
I was made to look the fool so that others would gather and see.

Many would say, "Are his changes really legit?
I see a fool loving God when he should quit.
He is proclaiming love for God up above
While he lives a life void of love.
He has a nice car and a home,
But he spends all his time alone.
You can tell that he's dying on the inside.
He probably uses God to hide.
But I'm going to watch this fool to the bitter end,
Because things always fall apart when people pretend."

That's when the Lord struck the match
That turned up the heat and made His plan hatch.
He said, "Thank you, son, for your service. It was faithful and true.
Now, I'm going to show them that you did everything I told you to.
You faced daily pressures, and others gave you another choice,
But you always stuck to the sound of My voice.
The one thing that sets you apart
Is that you recognize that people speak to your ears,
while I speak to your heart."

Not by Sight

Faith is not based on what we can see.
It is trusting the Lord Jesus with what will be.
It's putting our anxieties to rest
And let Jesus do what He does best.

In times of adversity, God is sometimes hated.
But don't forget: He's the Creator; we are the created.
So, before you shower Him with abuse,
Remember that the Potter made some pots for special use.

We are His pots crafted from clay,
And the LORD God gives and takes away.
Plus, being a child of the Almighty God
Won't spare us from His disciplinary rod.

Here's one more thing we can't afford to forget:
Having faith doesn't mean we'll enjoy what we get.

So Much

There is only so much I can see
Because some things are not revealed to me.
There is only so much for me to hear
Because there are some things the Lord will not share.

There is only so much Jesus will let me know,
Yet He gives enough for me to grow.
There is only so much I can take,
But God knows when to give me a break.

Having faith goes beyond what I can hear and see.
Even blinded and deaf, I have faith that the Lord
will fulfill His promises to me.

Stop

My heart pounds and fills with blood,
Thanks to an emotional flood.
My eyes fill with tears
As I realize my greatest fears.
My lips are parched and dry.
My thirst for you is why.
My skin boils and begins to burn
Because of for what I yearn.
My legs slowly wither away
From searching for you night and day.
I'm weak and I'm about to drop.
Then the Lord says, "I've got this. You can stop."

Details

Don't for a second think that God fails
When He doesn't give you the details.
He never reveals His entire plan
So that He can test the faith of man.
The things He withholds that cause a drought
Will one day come from His spout.
With His blessings, Jesus will give you a shower
To demonstrate His grace and awesome power.

Rusted Hope

Sometimes, God tells us that things will turn out great,
But He doesn't tell us about the painful wait.
Yet, we must give Him our trust
Even if our hope begins to rust.

No Doubt

Dear Lord Jesus, I don't doubt You.
After all, Your name is "Faithful and True".

ABOUT THE AUTHOR

Author photo by Sterlin King

Kollin L. Taylor went through a heartbreaking experience that brought him closer to God (his ultimate source of strength and inspiration), and launched his writing career. Within eighteen months, the Lord inspired him to write more than thirteen hundred poems and he published twenty-eight books. Therefore, Chaplain Robert A. Miller calls him *The Phenom*.

Kollin shares life lessons to enrich your soul in the following books:

Exposed Part I: The Prelude
Exposed Part II: Romantic Relationships
Exposed Part III: Vida
Exposed Part IV: The Journey Continues
Metamorphosis: The New Me
The Phenom: From My Soul
Resilience: Bend, Don't Break
The Aftermath: When the Smoke Clears and the Dust Settles
Perspective: A New Point of View
The Anatomy of a Heartbreak: When SAMson Met Delilah (autobiography)
Round 2: The Battle Continues
Round 3: Still Fighting
Cool Breeze: Irie Man
Finding Joy in You: The Gift of Eternal Life

Minister to the People: Answering His Calling
The Path to Enlightenment
Knowledge Is Power: Before You Do What You're Told, Know What You're Being Told
Soul Food: Thanks, Lord, for My Daily Bread
Closet Christian: If You Deny Him, He Will Deny You
Australia: A Journey Down Under
Wrongfully Accused: When Innocence Is Not Enough
The Sidelines: Those Who Can . . . .
Flirting with Disaster
The Sound of a Fallen Tree
Survival
Humble Pie: A Gift from God
Second Chances: Worthy of Redemption
God's Kitchen: His Slow-Cooked Stew
On Trial: A Test of My Faith is Kollin L. Taylor's twenty-ninth book and his twenty-eighth poetry book.

Connect with the author on Facebook at **https:// www.facebook.com/KollinLTaylor**

Printed in the United States
by Baker & Taylor Publisher Services